HAPPY Retirement

By Divine Stationaries

Name _____

Message _____

_____

_____

Email / Phone _____

Name _____

Message _____

_____

_____

Email / Phone _____

Name _____

Message _____

_____

_____

Email / Phone _____

Sit back and relax and do the things you never got a chance to do.
Julie Hebert

Name _____

Message _____

_____

_____

Email / Phone _____

Name _____

Message _____

_____

_____

Email / Phone _____

Name _____

Message _____

_____

_____

Email / Phone _____

**The idea that retirement is the reward for our many years of dedicated service is a
very contemporary perspective.** ___*Pamela J. Thomas*

Name _____

Message _____

_____

_____

Email / Phone _____

Name _____

Message _____

_____ , _____

_____

Email / Phone _____

Name _____

Message _____

_____

_____

Email / Phone _____

The more emotional investment we put into the people around us, the more quality of life and longevity surrounds us.   __*Lee Johnson*

Name _____

Message _____

_____

_____

Email / Phone _____

Name _____

Message _____

_____

_____

Email / Phone _____

Name _____

Message _____

_____

_____

Email / Phone _____

Don't cry because it's over, smile because it happened.
__Dr.Seuss

Name _____

Message _____

_____

_____

Email / Phone _____

Name _____

Message _____

_____

_____

Email / Phone _____

Name _____

Message _____

_____

_____

Email / Phone _____

How lucky I am to have something that makes saying goodbye so hard.

__Winnie the Pooh

Name _____

Message _____

_____

_____

Email / Phone _____

Name _____

Message _____

_____

_____

Email / Phone _____

Name _____

Message _____

_____

_____

Email / Phone _____

Aging seems to be the only available way to live a long life. --*Kitty O'Neill Collins*

Name _____

Message _____

_____

_____

Email / Phone _____

Name _____

Message _____

_____

_____

Email / Phone _____

Name _____

Message _____

_____

_____

Email / Phone _____

There is a whole new kind of life ahead, full of experiences just waiting to happen.
Some call it "retirement" I call it bliss.__ *Betty Sullivan*

Name _____

Message _____

_____

_____

Email / Phone _____

Name _____

Message _____

_____

_____

Email / Phone _____

Name _____

Message _____

_____

_____

Email / Phone _____

Do not just go through the day without pausing to ponder! You shall only retire wondering. ___*Agyemang Yeboah*

Name _____

Message _____

_____

_____

Email / Phone _____

Name _____

Message _____

_____

_____

Email / Phone _____

Name _____

Message _____

_____

_____

Email / Phone _____

**Middle age is when work is a lot less fun and fun is a lot more work. __*Unknown*

Name _____

Message _____

_____

_____

Email / Phone _____

Name _____

Message _____

_____

_____

Email / Phone _____

Name _____

Message _____

_____

_____

Email / Phone _____

**Retirement can be a great joy if you can figure out how to spend time without spending money. ___*Unknown*

Name _____

Message _____

_____

_____

Email / Phone _____

Name _____

Message _____

_____

_____

Email / Phone _____

Name _____

Message _____

_____

_____

Email / Phone _____

**If people concentrated on the really important things in life,
there'd be a shortage of fishing poles. __*Doug Larson***

Name _____

Message _____

_____

_____

Email / Phone _____

Name _____

Message _____

_____

_____

Email / Phone _____

Name _____

Message _____

_____

_____

Email / Phone _____

**Retirement is wonderful. It's doing nothing
without worrying about getting caught at it.** *Gene Perret*

Name _____

Message _____

_____

_____

Email / Phone _____

Name _____

Message _____

_____

_____

Email / Phone _____

Name _____

Message _____

_____

_____

Email / Phone _____

Retirement has been a discovery of beauty for me. I never had the time before to notice the beauty of my grandkids, my wife, the tree outside my very own front door. And, the beauty of time itself. __*Hartman Jule*__

Name _____

Message _____

_____

_____

Email / Phone _____

Name _____

Message _____

_____

_____

Email / Phone _____

Name _____

Message _____

_____

_____

Email / Phone _____

**Don't act your age in retirement. Act like the inner
young person you have always been.**
___John Anthony West_

Name _____

Message _____

_____

_____

Email / Phone _____

Name _____

Message _____

_____

_____

Email / Phone _____

Name _____

Message _____

_____

_____

Email / Phone _____

And in the end it's not the years in your life that count. It's the life in your years.
___*Abraham Lincoln*

Name _____

Message _____

_____

_____

Email / Phone _____

Name _____

Message _____

_____

_____

Email / Phone _____

Name _____

Message _____

_____

_____

Email / Phone _____

**The concept of freedom is never truly realized until one
settles into retirement mode. __*A. Major*

Name _____

Message _____

_____

_____

Email / Phone _____

Name _____

Message _____

_____

_____

Email / Phone _____

Name _____

Message _____

_____

_____

Email / Phone _____

**Retirement is wonderful if you have two essentials –
much to live on and much to live for.   __*Unknown***

Name _____

Message _____

_____

_____

Email / Phone _____

Name _____

Message _____

_____

_____

Email / Phone _____

Name _____

Message _____

_____

_____

Email / Phone _____

**There are some who start their retirement long
before they stop working.** _*Robert Half*

Name _____

Message _____

_____

_____

Email / Phone _____

Name _____

Message _____

_____

_____

Email / Phone _____

Name _____

Message _____

_____

_____

Email / Phone _____

**Retirement, a time to enjoy all the things you never had time
to do when you worked. _*Catherine Pulsifer***

Name _____

Message _____

_____

_____

Email / Phone _____

Name _____

Message _____

_____

_____

Email / Phone _____

Name _____

Message _____

_____

_____

Email / Phone _____

Retirement may be an ending, a closing, but it is also a new beginning.
_Catherine Pulsifer

Name _____

Message _____

_____

_____

Email / Phone _____

Name _____

Message _____

_____

_____

Email / Phone _____

Name _____

Message _____

_____

_____

Email / Phone _____

Best wishes on your retirement. Enjoy a rest that's overdue. Take pleasure in the finer things that are awaiting you. _*Judith Wibberley*

Name _____

Message _____

_____

_____

Email / Phone _____

Name _____

Message _____

_____

_____

Email / Phone _____

Name _____

Message _____

_____

_____

Email / Phone _____

I'm now as free as the breeze….. with roughly the same income. __Gene Perret

Name _____

Message _____

_____

_____

Email / Phone _____

Name _____

Message _____

_____

_____

Email / Phone _____

Name _____

Message _____

_____

_____

Email / Phone _____

There's never enough time to do all the nothing you want.
Bill Watterson, Calvin and Hobbes

Name _____

Message _____

_____

_____

Email / Phone _____

Name _____

Message _____

_____

_____

Email / Phone _____

Name _____

Message _____

_____

_____

Email / Phone _____

The trouble with retirement is that you never get a day off. __*Abe Lemons*

Name _____

Message _____

_____

_____

Email / Phone _____

Name _____

Message _____

_____

_____

Email / Phone _____

Name _____

Message _____

_____

_____

Email / Phone _____

**Choose a work that you love and you won't have to work another day. __*Confucius*

Name _____

Message _____

_____

_____

Email / Phone _____

Name _____

Message _____

_____

_____

Email / Phone _____

Name _____

Message _____

_____

_____

Email / Phone _____

It is better to live rich than to die rich. ___*Samuel Johnson*

Name _____

Message _____

_____

_____

Email / Phone _____

Name _____

Message _____

_____

_____

Email / Phone _____

Name _____

Message _____

_____

_____

Email / Phone _____

Not having to worry about money is almost like not having to worry about dying. *Mario Puzo*

Name _____

Message _____

_____

_____

Email / Phone _____

Name _____

Message _____

_____

_____

Email / Phone _____

Name _____

Message _____

_____

_____

Email / Phone _____

**Retired is being twice tired. I've thought, first tired of working,
then tired of not. __*Richard Armour***

Name _____

Message _____

_____

_____

Email / Phone _____

Name _____

Message _____

_____

_____

Email / Phone _____

Name _____

Message _____

_____

_____

Email / Phone _____

A retired husband is often a wife's full-time job. __*Ella Harris*

Name _____

Message _____

_____

_____

Email / Phone _____

Name _____

Message _____

_____

_____

Email / Phone _____

Name _____

Message _____

_____

_____

Email / Phone _____

A man is known by the company that keeps him

after retirement age. _ _*Unknown*

Name _____

Message _____

_____

_____

Email / Phone _____

Name _____

Message _____

_____

_____

Email / Phone _____

Name _____

Message _____

_____

_____

Email / Phone _____

It is time I stepped aside for a less experienced and less able man. __*Scott Elledge***

Name _____

Message _____

_____

_____

Email / Phone _____

Name _____

Message _____

_____

_____

Email / Phone _____

Name _____

Message _____

_____

_____

Email / Phone _____

**Half our life is spent trying to find something to do with the time we have
rushed through life trying to save. __ *Will Rogers***

Name _____

Message _____

_____

_____

Email / Phone _____

Name _____

Message _____

_____

_____

Email / Phone _____

Name _____

Message _____

_____

_____

Email / Phone _____

Retire from work, but not from life. __*M.K Soni*

Name _____

Message _____

_____

_____

Email / Phone _____

Name _____

Message _____

_____

_____

Email / Phone _____

Name _____

Message _____

_____

_____

Email / Phone _____

You are only young once, but you can stay immature indefinitely. *__Ogden Nash*

Name _____

Message _____

_____

_____

Email / Phone _____

Name _____

Message _____

_____

_____

Email / Phone _____

Name _____

Message _____

_____

_____

Email / Phone _____

Retirement is when you stop living at work and start working at living
- Unknown

Name _____

Message _____

_____

_____

Email / Phone _____

Name _____

Message _____

_____

_____

Email / Phone _____

Name _____

Message _____

_____

_____

Email / Phone _____

Retirement is the ugliest word in the language. __*Ernest Heminway*

Name _____

Message _____

_____

_____

Email / Phone _____

Name _____

Message _____

_____

_____

Email / Phone _____

Name _____

Message _____

_____

_____

Email / Phone _____

The money's no better in retirement but the hours are! __*Terri Guillemets*

Name _____

Message _____

_____

_____

Email / Phone _____

Name _____

Message _____

_____

_____

Email / Phone _____

Name _____

Message _____

_____

_____

Email / Phone _____

It appears history is going to keep happening, despite our hopes for retirement.
__*Gregory Maguire*__

Name _____

Message _____

_____

_____

Email / Phone _____

Name _____

Message _____

_____

_____

Email / Phone _____

Name _____

Message _____

_____

_____

Email / Phone _____

Retirement itself is the best gift. No gold watch could ever top it.
__Abigail Charleson

Name _____

Message _____

_____

_____

Email / Phone _____

Name _____

Message _____

_____

_____

Email / Phone _____

Name _____

Message _____

_____

_____

Email / Phone _____

When you retire, think and act as if you were still working; When you're still working, think and act a bit as if you were already retired. __Unknown

Name _____

Message _____

_____

_____

Email / Phone _____

Name _____

Message _____

_____

_____

Email / Phone _____

Name _____

Message _____

_____

_____

Email / Phone _____

Even If I don't reach all my goals, I've gone higher than I would have if I hadn't set any. __*Danielle Fotopoulis*

Name _____

Message _____

_____

_____

Email / Phone _____

Name _____

Message _____

_____

_____

Email / Phone _____

Name _____

Message _____

_____

_____

Email / Phone _____

**Feeling grateful or appreciative of someone or something in your life
actually attracts more of the things that you appreciate and value into your life.**
__Christiane Northrup

Name _____

Message _____

_____

_____

Email / Phone _____

Name _____

Message _____

_____

_____

Email / Phone _____

Name _____

Message _____

_____

_____

Email / Phone _____

It is one of the most beautiful compensations of life, that no man can
sincerely try to help another without helping himself.
___*Ralph Waldo*

Name _____

Message _____

_____

_____

Email / Phone _____

Name _____

Message _____

_____

_____

Email / Phone _____

Name _____

Message _____

_____

_____

Email / Phone _____

**Love grows by giving. The love we give away is the only love we keep.
The only way to retain love is to give it away. __*Edward Hubbard***

Name _____

Message _____

_____

_____

Email / Phone _____

Name _____

Message _____

_____

_____

Email / Phone _____

Name _____

Message _____

_____

_____

Email / Phone _____

**Enjoy every retirement day as if it was your last and
one day you will be right about it.** __*Unknown*

Name _____

Message _____

_____

_____

Email / Phone _____

Name _____

Message _____

_____

_____

Email / Phone _____

Name _____

Message _____

_____

_____

Email / Phone _____

Stay young at heart, kind in spirit, and enjoy retirement living.
__Danielle Duckery

Name _____

Message _____

_____

_____

Email / Phone _____

Name _____

Message _____

_____

_____

Email / Phone _____

Name _____

Message _____

_____

_____

Email / Phone _____

I have found that if you love life, life will love you back.
___Arthur Rubinstein

Name _____

Message _____

_____

_____

Email / Phone _____

Name _____

Message _____

_____

_____

Email / Phone _____

Name _____

Message _____

_____

_____

Email / Phone _____

Let today be a day to face life with courage, with faith, and with a light heart.
___*Jonathan Lockwood Huie*___

Name _____

Message _____

_____

_____

Email / Phone _____

Name _____

Message _____

_____

_____

Email / Phone _____

Name _____

Message _____

_____

_____

Email / Phone _____

**The unselfish effort to bring cheer to others will be the beginning
of a happier life for ourselves. __*Helen Keller*

Name _____

Message _____

_____

_____

Email / Phone _____

Name _____

Message _____

_____

_____

Email / Phone _____

Name _____

Message _____

_____

_____

Email / Phone _____

Where there is great love there are always miracle.
___ *Willa Cather*

Name _____

Message _____

_____

_____

Email / Phone _____

Name _____

Message _____

_____

_____

Email / Phone _____

Name _____

Message _____

_____

_____

Email / Phone _____

Wisdom is to live in the present, plan for the future and profit from the past.
_Unknown

Name _____

Message _____

_____

_____

Email / Phone _____

Name _____

Message _____

_____

_____

Email / Phone _____

Name _____

Message _____

_____

_____

Email / Phone _____

Never give up. Expect only the best from life and take action to get it.
___Catherine Pulsifer

Name _____

Message _____

_____

_____

Email / Phone _____

Name _____

Message _____

_____

_____

Email / Phone _____

Name _____

Message _____

_____

_____

Email / Phone _____

When you're at the end of your rope, tie a knot and hold on.
___Theodore Roosevelt

Name _____

Message _____

_____

_____

Email / Phone _____

Name _____

Message _____

_____

_____

Email / Phone _____

Name _____

Message _____

_____

_____

Email / Phone _____

**In order to succeed, your desire for success should be greater than you fear of failure. __*Bill Cosby*

Name _____

Message _____

_____

_____

Email / Phone _____

Name _____

Message _____

_____

_____

Email / Phone _____

Name _____

Message _____

_____

_____

Email / Phone _____

Accept responsibility for your life. Know that it is you who will get you where you want to go, no one else. __ *Les Brown*

Name _____

Message _____

_____

_____

Email / Phone _____

Name _____

Message _____

_____

_____

Email / Phone _____

Name _____

Message _____

_____

_____

Email / Phone _____

Challenges are what makes life interesting and overcoming them is what makes life meaningful. __*Joshua J. Marine*

Name _____

Message _____

_____

_____

Email / Phone _____

Name _____

Message _____

_____

_____

Email / Phone _____

Name _____

Message _____

_____

_____

Email / Phone _____

**The trick is to enjoy life. Don't wish away your days,
waiting for better ones ahead.__ *Marjorie Pay Hinckley***

Name _____

Message _____

_____

_____

Email / Phone _____

Name _____

Message _____

_____

_____

Email / Phone _____

Name _____

Message _____

_____

_____

Email / Phone _____

Go confidently in the direction of your dreams. Live the life you have imagined.
__*Henry DavidThoreau*__

Name _____

Message _____

_____

_____

Email / Phone _____

Name _____

Message _____

_____

_____

Email / Phone _____

Name _____

Message _____

_____

_____

Email / Phone _____

If you try, you risk failure. If you don't, you ensure it.
__Anonymous

Name _____

Message _____

_____

_____

Email / Phone _____

Name _____

Message _____

_____

_____

Email / Phone _____

Name _____

Message _____

_____

_____

Email / Phone _____

Life is what happens to us while we are making other plans.
___Allen Saunders

Name _____

Message _____

_____

_____

Email / Phone _____

Name _____

Message _____

_____

_____

Email / Phone _____

Name _____

Message _____

_____

_____

Email / Phone _____

You only live once, but if you do it right, once is enough.
__Mae West

Name _____

Message _____

_____

_____

Email / Phone _____

Name _____

Message _____

_____

_____

Email / Phone _____

Name _____

Message _____

_____

_____

Email / Phone _____

Don't start your day with the broken pieces of yesterday. Every morning
we wake up is the first day of the rest of our life - Unkno

Name _____

Message _____

_____

_____

Email / Phone _____

Name _____

Message _____

_____

_____

Email / Phone _____

Name _____

Message _____

_____

_____

Email / Phone _____

As you embark on the exciting journey into retirement, you will experience a transition that will be both thrilling and terrifying. __Olivia Green

Name _____

Message _____

_____

_____

Email / Phone _____

Name _____

Message _____

_____

_____

Email / Phone _____

Name _____

Message _____

_____

_____

Email / Phone _____

You have to do your thing no matter what anyone says. It's your life.
___Ethan Embry

Name _____

Message _____

_____

_____

Email / Phone _____

Name _____

Message _____

_____

_____

Email / Phone _____

Name _____

Message _____

_____

_____

Email / Phone _____

Live Laugh and Love - Unknown

Name _____

Message _____

_____

_____

Email / Phone _____

Name _____

Message _____

_____

_____

Email / Phone _____

Name _____

Message _____

_____

_____

Email / Phone _____

**Men can only be happy when they do not assume
that the object of life is happiness.** __*George Orwell*

Name _____

Message _____

_____

_____

Email / Phone _____

Name _____

Message _____

_____

_____

Email / Phone _____

Name _____

Message _____

_____

_____

Email / Phone _____

Success is not the key to happiness. Happiness is the key to success.
If you love what you are doing, you will be successful.
__*Albert Shweitzer*

Name _____

Message _____

_____

_____

Email / Phone _____

Name _____

Message _____

_____

_____

Email / Phone _____

Name _____

Message _____

_____

_____

Email / Phone _____

**I do not exist to impress the world. I exist to live my life
in a way that will make me happy. ___*Richard Bach***

Name _____

Message _____

_____

_____

Email / Phone _____

Name _____

Message _____

_____

_____

Email / Phone _____

Name _____

Message _____

_____

_____

Email / Phone _____

Learn how to be happy with what you have while you pursue all that you want.
__Jim Rohn

Name _____

Message _____

_____

_____

Email / Phone _____

Name _____

Message _____

_____

_____

Email / Phone _____

Name _____

Message _____

_____

_____

Email / Phone _____

The brave may not live forever, but the cautious don't live at all.
__Ashley J.

Name _____

Message _____

_____

_____

Email / Phone _____

Name _____

Message _____

_____

_____

Email / Phone _____

Name _____

Message _____

_____

_____

Email / Phone _____

**The only thing that stands between you and your dream is the will to try
and the belief that it is actually possible.   - Joel Brown**

Name _____

Message _____

_____

_____

Email / Phone _____

Name _____

Message _____

_____

_____

Email / Phone _____

Name _____

Message _____

_____

_____

Email / Phone _____

The pain you feel today is the strength you feel tomorrow. For every challenge encountered there is opportunity for growth. __*Unknown*

Name _____

Message _____

_____

_____

Email / Phone _____

Name _____

Message _____

_____

_____

Email / Phone _____

Name _____

Message _____

_____

_____

Email / Phone _____

The only way to do great work is to love what you do. If you haven't found it yet. Keep looking. Don't settle. ___*Steve Jobs*

Name _____

Message _____

_____

_____

Email / Phone _____

Name _____

Message _____

_____

_____

Email / Phone _____

Name _____

Message _____

_____

_____

Email / Phone _____

Don't be afraid to stand for what you believe in, even if that means standing alone. __Andy Biersack

Name _____

Message _____

_____

_____

Email / Phone _____

Name _____

Message _____

_____

_____

Email / Phone _____

Name _____

Message _____

_____

_____

Email / Phone _____

**I think the notion of retirement is just a dreadful, dreadful idea
and I hope I never have to do that. __*Michael Moritz***

Name _____

Message _____

_____

_____

Email / Phone _____

Name _____

Message _____

_____

_____

Email / Phone _____

Name _____

Message _____

_____

_____

Email / Phone _____

Don't limit yourself. Many people limit themselves to what they think they can do.
You can go as far as your mind lets you. What you believe you can achieve.
_Mary Kay Ash

Name _____

Message _____

_____

_____

Email / Phone _____

Name _____

Message _____

_____

_____

Email / Phone _____

Name _____

Message _____

_____

_____

Email / Phone _____

Happiness is a risk. If you're not a little scared, then you're not doing it right.
        __Sarah Addison Allen

Name _____

Message _____

_____

_____

Email / Phone _____

Name _____

Message _____

_____

_____

Email / Phone _____

Name _____

Message _____

_____

_____

Email / Phone _____

We make a living by what we get. We make a life by what we give.
__Winston Churchill

Name _____

Message _____

_____

_____

Email / Phone _____

Name _____

Message _____

_____

_____

Email / Phone _____

Name _____

Message _____

_____

_____

Email / Phone _____

Often when you think you're at the end of something, you're at the beginning of something else. _Fred Rogers

Gift Log

DATE	GIFT DESCRIPTION	GIVEN BY	THANK YOU NOTICE SENT

Gift Log

DATE	GIFT DESCRIPTION	GIVEN BY	THANK YOU NOTICE SENT

Gift Log

DATE	GIFT DESCRIPTION	GIVEN BY	THANK YOU NOTICE SENT

Gift Log

DATE	GIFT DESCRIPTION	GIVEN BY	THANK YOU NOTICE SENT

Gift Log

DATE	GIFT DESCRIPTION	GIVEN BY	THANK YOU NOTICE SENT

Gift Log

DATE	GIFT DESCRIPTION	GIVEN BY	THANK YOU NOTICE SENT

Made in the USA
Coppell, TX
10 April 2021

53381485R00057